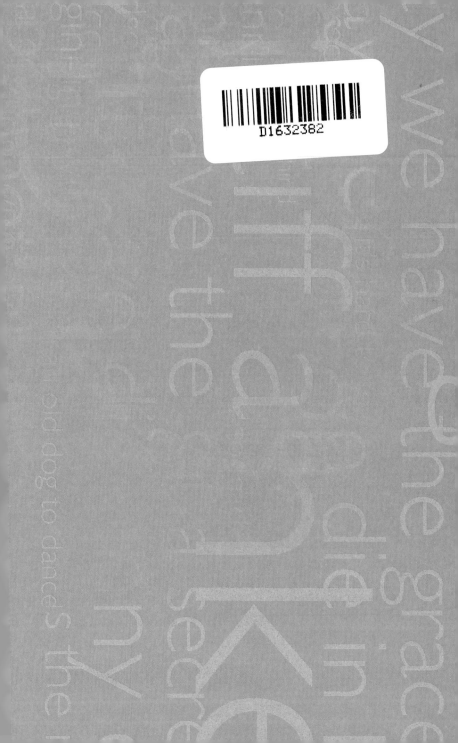
we have the
die in
the
old dog to dance
D1632382

IRISH PROVERBS & SAYINGS

'May the Lord keep you in his hand and never close his fist too tight on you'

Seamus Cashman is a poet and former book publisher – he founded the Irish literary publishing house Wolfhound Press in 1974. He has had several volumes of poetry published, including *That Morning will Come: New and Selected Poems* (2007) and *The Sistine Gaze: I too begin with scaffolding* (2015), both by Salmon Poetry (www.salmonpoetry.com). Now living in Swords, Co Dublin, he comes from the village of Conna in County Cork.

Sean Gaffney, who died in 2017, worked in telecommunications in Dublin for many years before retiring to his home town of Cavan.

IRISH PROVERBS & SAYINGS

SEAMUS CASHMAN & SEAN GAFFNEY

THE O'BRIEN PRESS
DUBLIN

This edition first published 2019 by
The O'Brien Press Ltd,
12 Terenure Road East, Rathgar, D06 HD27, Dublin 6, Ireland.
Tel: +353 1 4923333; Fax: +353 1 4922777
E-mail: books@obrien.ie
Website: www.obrien.ie
First published 1974 by Wolfhound Press.
Updated edition published 2015 by The O'Brien Press.
The O'Brien Press is a member of Publishing Ireland.

ISBN: 978-1-78849-041-2

5 4 3 2 1
23 22 21 20 19

Printed and bound by Gutenberg Press, Malta.
The paper in this book is produced using pulp from managed forests.

Published in

CONTENTS

Irish Wolfhounds

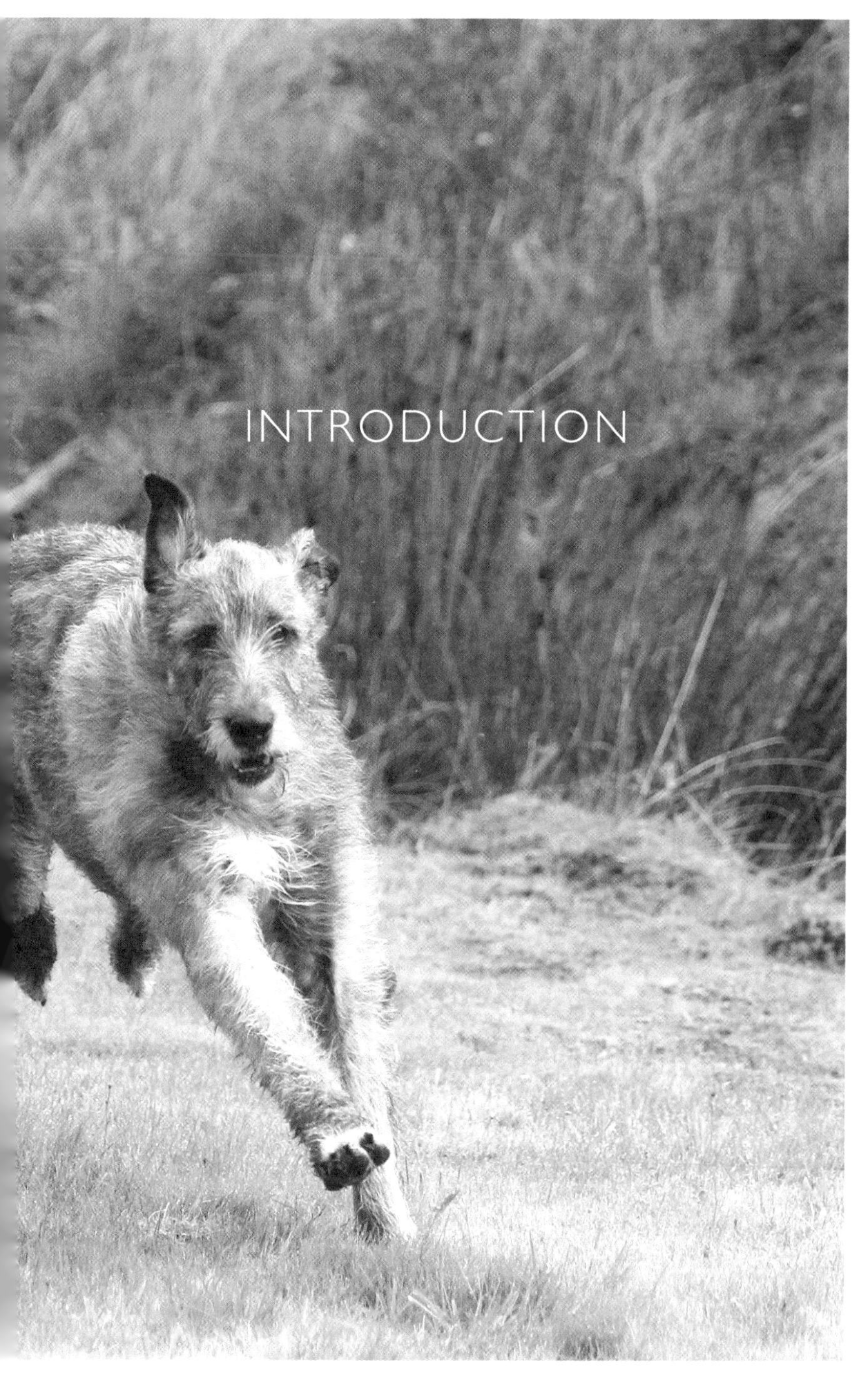

INTRODUCTION

'The proverb cannot be bettered'; 'though the proverb is abandoned, it cannot be falsified'. How true these are readers will best discover for themselves in the following collection of Irish proverbs, sayings and triads. The triad is perhaps the most fascinating type of saying, and, though little heard today in the non-Irish-speaking parts of the country, it is still to be found in the Gaeltacht areas, especially in West Cork, West Galway and the Aran Islands.

A glance through the index of keywords reveals the range of the Irish proverb, its themes and the imagery and symbols used. As might be expected, the reputed vulnerability of our race to religion and romanticism is well represented. But the story the proverb tells is not quite that of a priest-ridden peasantry content in their poverty. Rather, it shows us to have – or at least to have had – a subtle, sly perhaps, but generally humorous self-confidence. 'The priest's pig' may get 'the most porridge', but the proverb also advises us to be 'neither intimate nor distant with the clergy'! Nor are we shown to be wholly susceptible to romanticism: 'it's better to be lucky than to be an early riser', but 'there's no success without authority and laws'. The proverbs reveal a deep conviction in a relationship between the spiritual and the material that is both challenging and realistic.

Proverbs are, in a sense, a race's unconscious expression of its moral attitudes. Our proverbs seem frequently to take the form of a national confession of sins: the evils of drink, gambling, greed, vanity, improvidence abound. But the virtues are there: faith, gentleness, love of nature, tolerance and a trust in a life after death that offers a constant check to the materialism already mentioned.

Irish proverbs are rich in nature symbolism and imagery: the wind, the sea, the mountains; plants, animals, birds and fishes. The kingfisher, mackerel, thistle, plover, the horse and the hare, even the common crow are all called upon to mirror our achievements, hopes and failings.

While the proverbs of a race are often readily identifiable as belonging to that race, the ideas expressed and the images used touch on matters more fundamental than a national identity. One can readily accept that Irish proverbs should have their exact counterparts among the proverbs of other Celtic races. There are numerous examples of similarities among the sayings of the Irish, Welsh and Scottish: 'A long illness doesn't lie' (Irish); 'To be long sick and to die nevertheless' (Welsh); 'Marriage at the dungheap and the godparents far away' (Irish); 'Marriage o'er the anvil, sponsorship o'er the sea' (Scottish); 'A drink is shorter than a story' (Irish and Manx); 'Bribery splits a stone' (Scottish). Such typical proverbs as these also have their counterparts in most European languages.

However, it is interesting to discover that our proverbs also have affinities with those of races as far distant as the West Indies and

Africa. Among Jamaicans of African descent, there is a saying: 'When you sleep wid darg, you ketch him flea.' Our equivalent is 'He who lies with dogs rises with fleas.' We speak of sending the goose on a message to the foxes' den; the Hausa of West Africa have 'Even if the hyena's town is destroyed, one does not send a dog in to trade.'

Irish proverbs and sayings derive from two mainstreams: the Gaelic tradition, in the Irish language, and the Anglo-Irish tradition, in the English language. Both reflect the strong biblical influence found in proverbs throughout 'Western' countries. This collection includes some of the oldest *seanfhocail* (old sayings) recorded in Ireland as well as sayings of more recent origin. But it is by no means exhaustive. The exact origins of most of these sayings are unknown: perhaps a throwaway phrase; perhaps a line of a poem long forgotten – who knows? It is what survives that matters.

For readers interested in pursuing the Irish proverb further, a brief word on some sources. Several substantial collections have been published (from which many in this collection have been taken, and which we gratefully acknowledge). Most of these are unfortunately long out of print. The most recent, and certainly the finest is T. S. O'Maille, ed., *Sean-fhocala Chonnacht*, 2 vols. (Dublin, 1948–52). Others are: T. O'Donoghue, ed., *Sean-fhocail na Mumhain*, a Gaelic League publication, 1902; E. Ua Muirgheasa, ed., *Sean fhocla Uladh* (1907), which contains English translations, as does T. F. O'Rahilly, *A Miscellany of Irish Proverbs* (Dublin, 1922). Shorter collections will be found in J. O'Daly, *Irish Language Miscellany*; Burke, *Irish Grammar*; Hardiman, *Irish Minstrelsy*, 2 vols., reissued by Irish University Press in 1969; the *Gaelic Journal* and *The Ulster Journal of Archaeology*. P. W. Joyce, *English as We Speak It in Ireland* (Dublin, 1910), is a useful and entertaining starting point though of limited use for proverbs. Two important sources still to be fully researched are the Douglas Hyde 'Diaries' in the National Library of Ireland and the manuscript collections of the Irish Folklore Department in UCD, in particular the 'Schools Mss.' for Anglo-Irish proverbs. *Béaloideas,* the journal of the Folklore Commission, includes lists of proverbs in its various issues. Information on further sources will be found in bibliographies in the published works mentioned.

Most of the proverbs in this collection have been translated from the Irish language. English translations of proverbs in the Irish language are not always successful. We have endeavoured to remain as close to the original as possible. An illustration of the effects of translation, however, can be readily seen by comparing 'One beetle recognises another' with the original Irish proverb, 'Aithníonn ciaróg ciaróg eile.' The impact of the expression depends greatly on the sound of the word *ciaróg*, and its repetition. The pattern cannot be reproduced satisfactorily in English; and the word 'beetle' is by comparison with the Irish word weak and ineffectual.

We have classified each proverb by subject, recognising that such classification is both limiting and subjective. Proverbs are by their very nature elusive and usually defy adequate classification under any one heading. However, as the index contains the keywords of each proverb, our arrangement should cause the reader little difficulty.

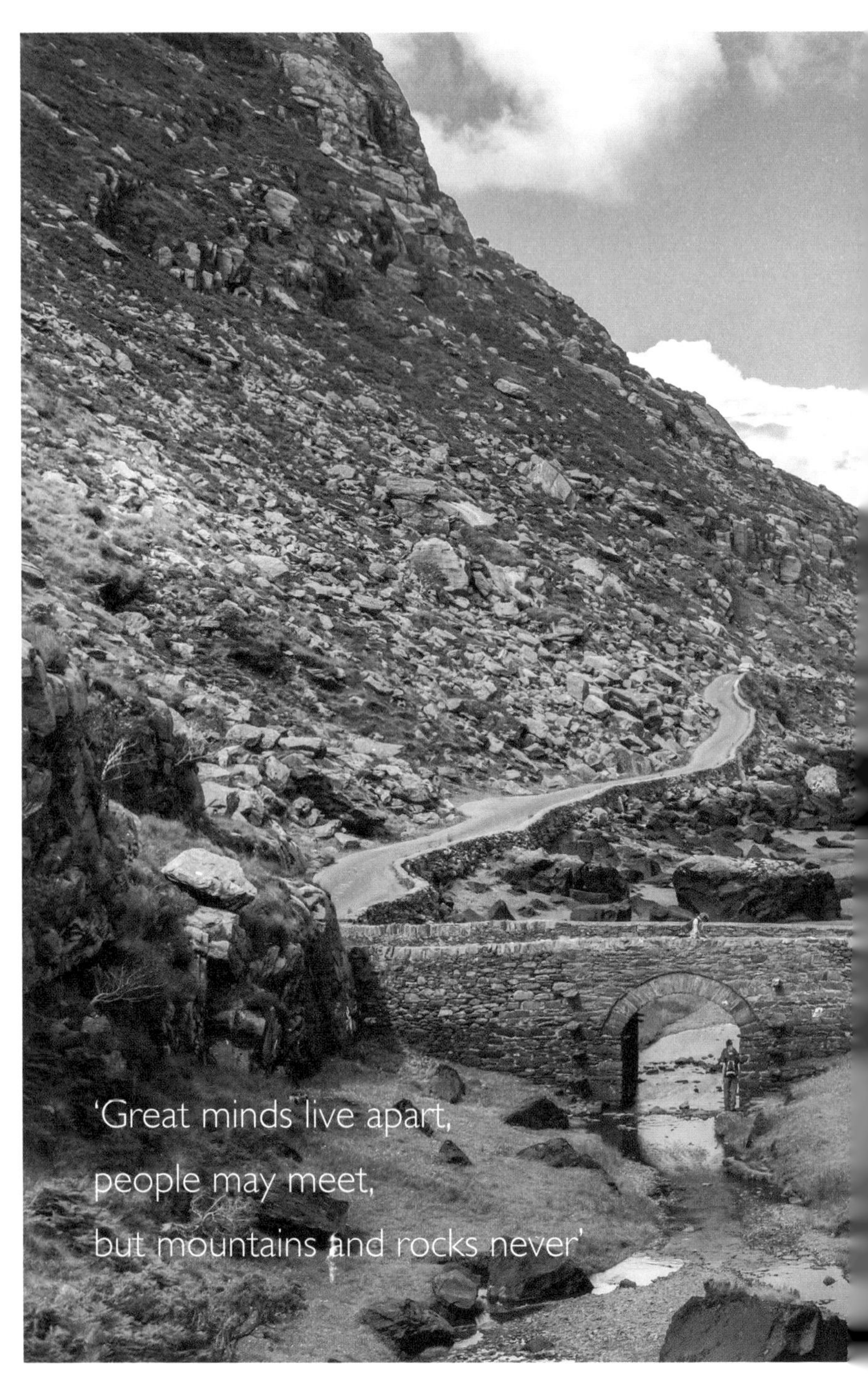
'Great minds live apart,
people may meet,
but mountains and rocks never'

CLASSIFICATIONS

Gap of Dunloe, County Kerry

'When the twig hardens,
it's difficult to twist it'
The Dark Hedges, County Antrim

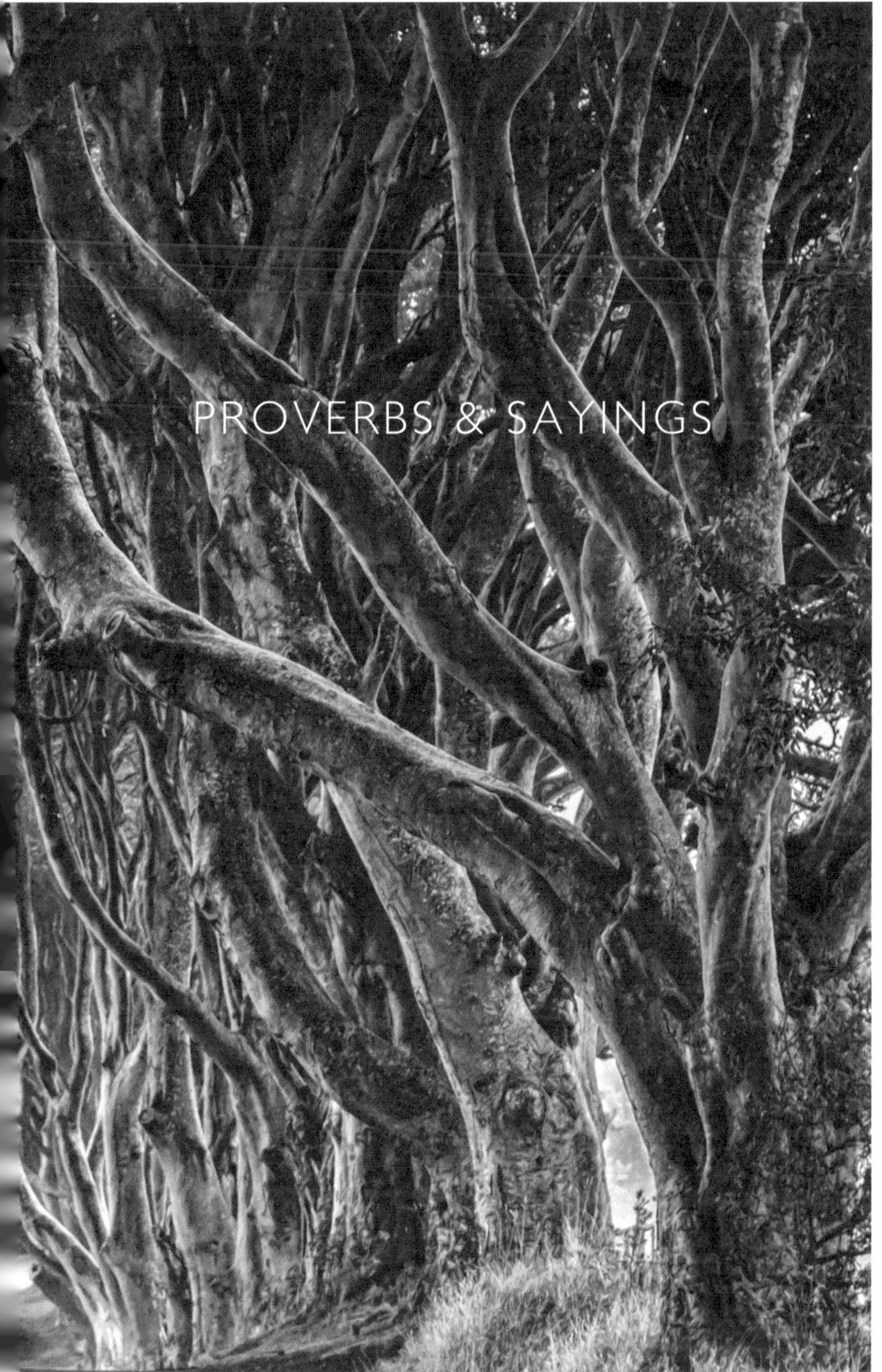

PROVERBS & SAYINGS

ABILITY

No one can tell what he is able to do till he tries no. 1

You can't whistle and chew meal at the same time 2

You can't bark and run at the same time 3

A vessel only holds its fill 4

Often the hound that was made fun of killed the deer 5

The strong man may when he wants to; the weak man when he's able 6

The *gobadán* (kingfisher) cannot work both tides 7

ADVICE

Don't give cherries to pigs; don't give advice to a fool 8

A man is often a bad adviser to himself and a good adviser to another 9

The man who won't have advice will have conflict 10

He is bad that will not take advice, but he is a thousand times worse that takes every advice 11

The cat is his own best adviser 12

Crafty advice is often got from a fool 13

A wise man takes advice 14

AFFECTATION

AGE

ANGER

APPEARANCE

ART

AS ... AS

As tough as a wheelstring 41

As mim as a dog without his tail 42

As black as Toal's cloak 43

As bad as Barrington's bloodhound to us 44

A localised Kerry expression. When the Irish were being hunted down in Penal times, a particularly vicious duo, a Captain Barrington and Colonel Nelson, used a bloodhound to chase their quarry which savaged the victim terribly, hence giving rise to the saying

As old as Atty Hayes' goat 45

A Cork expression. The story goes that the goat belonged to Atwell Hayes who was father of Sir Henry Hayes, sheriff of Cork in 1790. The goat was reputed to be old even when Atty was a young man. A generation later, Captain Philip Allen, son-in-law of Sir Henry Hayes became mayor of Cork (in 1800) and gave a civil banquet to celebrate the occasion. At this time the goat died, and Allen, being a bit of a joker, served up the hind quarters of the goat unknowingly to his guests, as venison. The 'venison' was proclaimed delicious by the city fathers. In County Armagh, the corresponding expression is 'as old as Killylea bog'

As wise as the woman of Mungret 46

A Limerick expression. The very amusing story attached to this saying concerns the monastic foundation and school at Mungret. A number of scholars were sent from Cashel to compete with their Mungret counterparts. However, the Limerick scholars, fearing defeat and the loss of their reputation, dressed as washerwomen and waited along the roadside,washing in the nearby river. As the Cashel contingent approached and asked the 'women' for directions, they were completely taken aback when answered in perfect Greek. Thinking that if the washerwomen were so learned then the scholars must be unusually brilliant, the poor Tipperary monks turned for home, leaving the reputation of Mungret intact and untarnished!

As true as the gospel 67

As deep as the sea 68

As bashful as a girl 69

As treacherous as an Englishman 70

As melodious as a lark 71

As brave as Fionn mac Cumhaill (*see notes*) 72

As yellow as a ragweed (ragworth) 73

As lazy as a donkey 74

As lazy as a piper's *luidín* (little finger) 75

As busy as a bee 76

As salty as the sea 77

As good as gold 78

As rich as Damer 79

A Dublin expression, not in common usage. The story is based on Joseph Damer who was born in 1630. After serving Cromwell he returned to Ireland where he purchased much land forfeited in the Williamite confiscations. He became a banker and achieved much notoriety as a miser. He died in 1720, leaving nearly half a million pounds, a phenomenal amount even by today's standards. Jonathan Swift was moved, as was his wont, to comment unfavourably on Mr. Damer:

The ghost of old Damer who left not his betters
When it heard of a bank appear'd to his debtors
And lent them for money the backs of his letters
His debtors they wonder'd to find him so frank,
For old Nick gave the papers the mark of the bank

BEAUTY

BETRAYER

BITTERNESS

BLESSINGS

BOASTING

BORROWING

BRAVERY

BRIBERY

CARELESSNESS

CAUTION

'Look at the river before you cross the ferry'

The River Shannon

CHANGE

CHARACTER

CHARITY

CHASTITY

CHILDREN

No man ever wore a cravat as nice as his own child's arm around his neck 170

Your son is your son today, but your daughter is your daughter forever 171

CHOICE

If the bare part of the hill is bad, the summit is worse 172

It can't be both curds and whey with you 173

It's difficult to choose between two blind goats 174

CLERGY

The priest's pig gets the most porridge 175

Although there was nobody present but the priest and the friar, still I have lost all my property 176

A dumb priest never got a parish 177

If there is a hen or a goose it's surely on the priest's table it will be 178

It is his own child the priest baptises first 179

Be neither intimate nor distant with the clergy 180

A priest that's made a pet of and a pig that's made a pet of are the two worst pets of all 181

The way of the nuns with the countrywomen – they receive a great lump and give a small return 182

Give the priest his own side of the road 183

COINCIDENCE

COMFORT

COMPROMISE

CONTENTMENT

CONVERSATION

COURTSHIP

CRITICISM

CUNNING

CURSES

CYNICISM

DANGER

DEATH

There is hope from the mouth of the sea but none from the mouth of the grave 227

A man at sea may return but not the man in the churchyard 228

Sleep is the brother (or the image) of death 229

One can't tell which skin will hang from the rafter first, the old sheep's or the lamb's 230

The trace of the hand will live but not the hand that made it 231

Death stares the old in the face and lurks behind the backs of the young 232

Nimble as the hare is, she is caught at last 233

There is many a person with a high head today who will be lying lowly tomorrow 234

May God spare anyone who has a hand in his own death 235

You will never comb a grey head 236

It is not the tree that is a long time shaking that is the first to fall 237

Death does not take a bribe 238

The graveyard growth is in him 239

Death never comes too late 240

You'll be going yet and your two feet before you 241

DEBT

DECEPTION

DELUSION

DESIRE

DESPAIR

DEVIL

DISCIPLINE

DISMISSAL

DRINK

It [whiskey] would make a rabbit spit at a dog 268

He would go to mass every morning if holy water were whiskey 269

You take your health once too often to the whiskey shop till it gets broken 270

It's sweet to drink but bitter to pay for it 271

Sweet is the wine but sour's the payment 272

Wine reveals the truth 273

Thirst after the drink and sorrow after the money 274

Drunkenness will not protect a secret 275

The cure of the drinking is to drink again 276

Thirst is a shameless disease 277

Donal drunk and his wife drinking water 278

He would drink Lough Sheelin dry (*see notes*) 279

It is only folly to treat an old woman to a dram 280

When good luck comes the drink comes 281

A drunken woman is lost to shame 282

Thirst begets thirst 283

The end of drinking is more thirst 284

ECONOMY

Take what you can get and pay what you can 285

EDUCATION

EFFORT

EGOTISM

ELOQUENCE

ENDURANCE

THE ENGLISH

EQUALITY

ERROR

EVIL

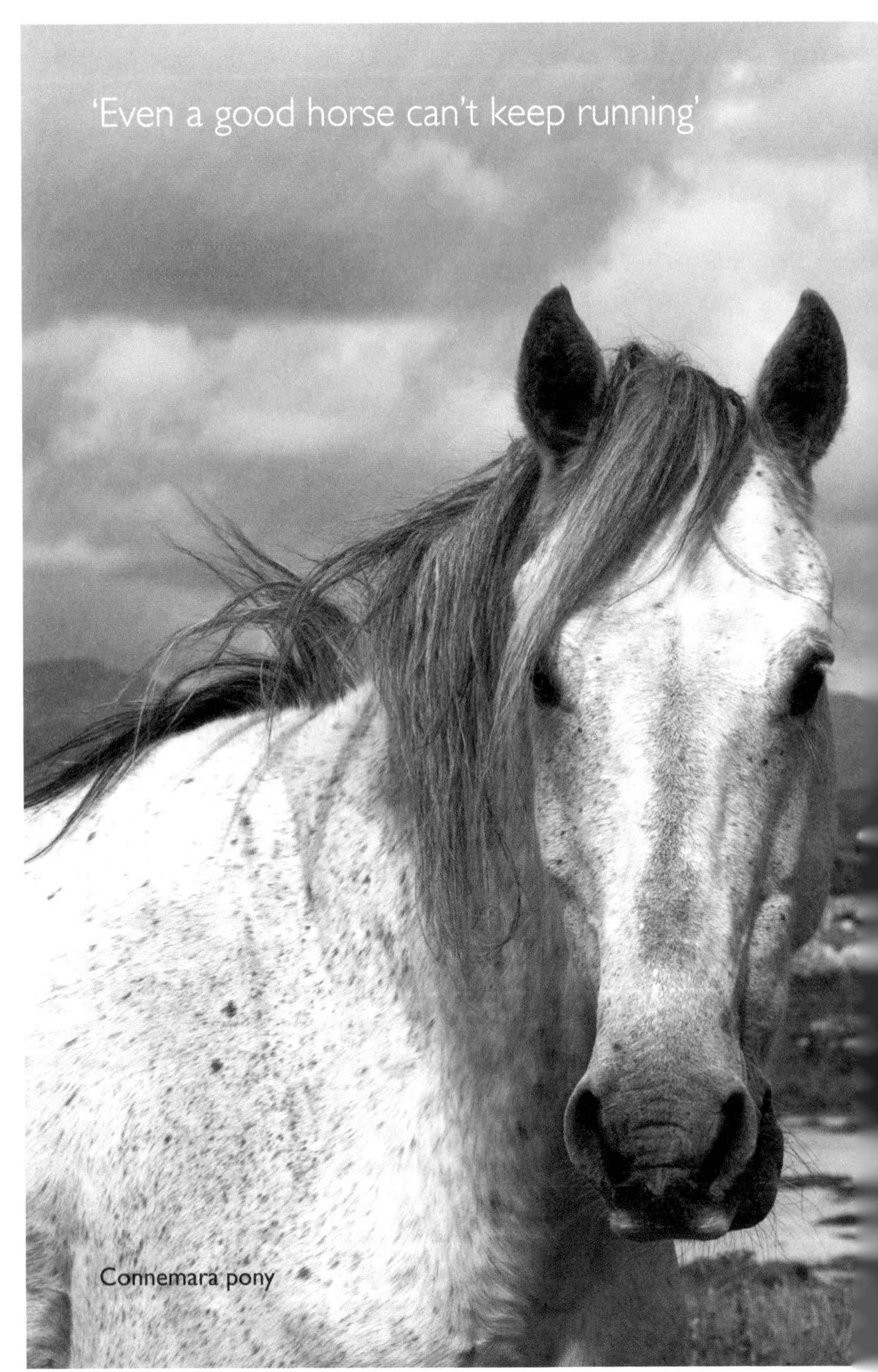
'Even a good horse can't keep running'

Connemara pony

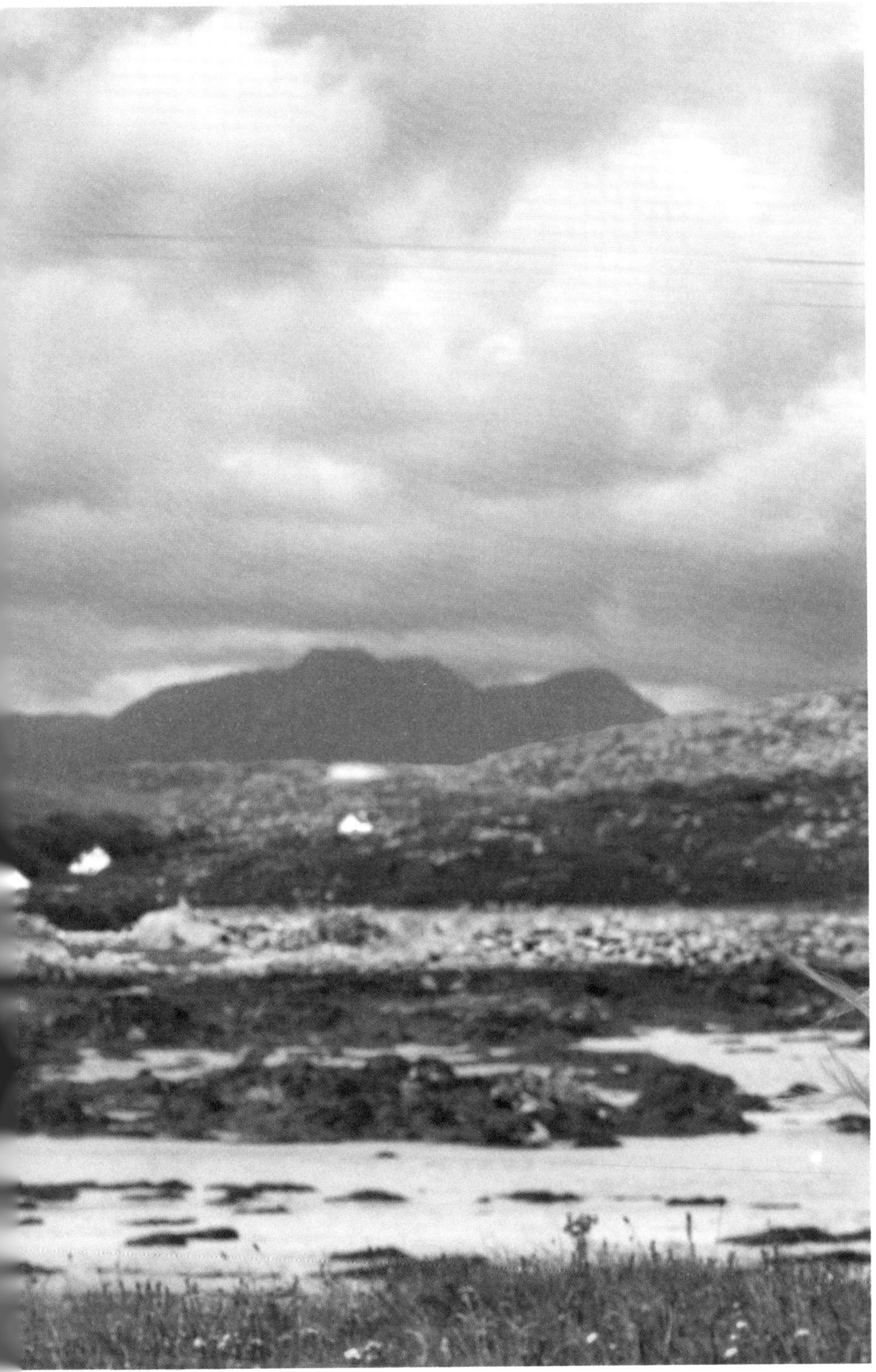

EXCUSES

EXPERIENCE

Sense bought (i.e. experience) is better than two senses learned 325

You can't put an old head on young shoulders 326

Every hound is a pup till he hunts 327

FAIR-HAIRED

If I am yellow I have a fair heart 328

FAME

Fame lasts longer than life 329

Without money fame is dead 330

Falling is easier than rising 331

Greatness knows modesty 332

FAMILIARITY

To know somebody, (one must) live in the same house with them 333

Too much of one thing is the same as nothing 334

Familiarity breeds contempt 335

People of the same trade are friendly 336

FATE

Long as the day may be, night comes at last 337

He that is born to be hanged needn't fear water 338

Every nursling as it is nursed, every web as it is woven 339

Pity the man drowned in the storm; for after the rain comes the sunshine 340

The darkest hour is nearest dawn 341

A ship is often lost by the harbour 342

No matter how often a pitcher goes to the water, it is broken in the end 343

No matter how long the day, night comes 344

What kills one man gives life to another 345

About the foot of the tree the foliage falls 346

FEAR

Fear is a fine spur; so is rage 347

Be afraid, and you'll not meet danger 348

The man who is struck on the head, will afterwards be afraid 349

FIGHTING

To fight like Kilkenny cats 350

In 1798 when the Hessians were quartered in Kilkenny they amused themselves by tying two cats' tails together and throwing them over a line, to fight. Their officer on hearing of this, ordered his men to stop. However, the soldiers continued the practice in secret, and one day while they were amusing themselves in this manner they heard the officer approaching. One soldier drawing his sword cut down the cats leaving only their tails hanging. When the officer enquired as to where the cats were, the soldier replied that the cats had fought so furiously they had devoured all but each other's tails. The story proved immensely popular and achieved widespread fame, but it is probably just a tall tale!

Quarrelsome dogs get dirty coats 351

Don't kick till you're spurred 352

Be warning but not striking 353

A word goes to the wind but a blow goes to the bones 354

Wine is better than blood 355

There is often the death of a person between two words 356

Don't go between the tree and its bark 357

FLATTERY

Soft words butter no parsnips 358

FLIMSINESS

The sheep could eat the grass through it 359

FOOD

The juice of the cow alive or dead is good 360

Help is a good thing except at the table of food 361

A man at the food and a weakling at the work 362

First at the pot and last at the work 363

FOOL

FOOLISHNESS

Don't take the thatch off your own house to buy slates for another man's roof 380

Folly has a fall before it 381

There are two things that cannot be cured: death, and want of sense 382

FORGIVENESS

Forgive a horse that will cock his ears 383

FORTUNE

Good luck is better than early rising 384

Fortune is a good thing, but it's worth searching for it 385

The ugly are often lucky and the handsome unfortunate 386

Often does the likely fail and the unlikely prosper 387

It is a bad wind that doesn't blow for someone 388

Prosperity often comes to the easygoing 389

The lucky man awaits prosperity, the unlucky man gives a blind leap 390

Let each person judge his own luck, good or bad 391

FRAIL

The point of a rush would draw blood from his cheek 392

FREEDOM

FRIENDSHIP

Take care but take no sides and on no account sacrifice your friends 408

Pick your company before you sit down 409

Tell me who your friends are and I'll tell you who you are 410

A friend in court is better than a penny in one's purse 411

Friendship is good though separation is painful 412

Cook a little spit for me and I'll cook one for you 413

As well whistle jigs to a milestone as tell troubles to you 414

Friends are better than gold 415

A constant guest is never welcome 416

Don't show your skin to the person who won't cover it 417

The people will meet but the hills and mountains never 418

The coldness of a friend is better than the sweetness of an enemy 419

He who lies with dogs rises with fleas 420

It is better to be alone than to be in bad company 421

Be kind with the wretched but dark and dour to your enemy 422

When the hand ceases to scatter, the mouth ceases to praise 423

A little help is better than a deal of pity 424

Don't put your friend in your pocket 425

A shoulder without a kinsman (friend) is bare, and woe to him who lacks a loving brother 426

Pity the man in a country where there is none to take his part 427

FUTILITY

Putting the thatch of the kiln on the mill 428

It's like looking for a hound without knowing its colour 429

To address a head without knowledge is like the barking of a dog in a green valley 430

You might as well talk to the wall as to him 431

Don't waste your breath on dead embers 432

A nod is as good as a wink to a blind horse 433

It's no use going to the goat's house to look for wool 434

It's hard to fight with the wide ocean 435

An empty bag won't stand 436

'Tis hard to drive a hare out of a bush he's not in 437

You can't draw blood out of a turnip 438

You won't make a rope from the sand of the sea 439

It's only the Lord can make a racehorse out of a jackass 440

The Devil couldn't do it unless he was drunk 441

'Tis no use talking when the harm is done 442

GAMBLING

It is the hope of recompense that ruins the card-player 443

Better a son a gambler than a drinker 444

The expectation of success is what beggars the gambler 445

GENEROSITY

A big belly was never generous 446

A generous man, they say, has never gone to Hell 447

Wide is the door of the little cottage 448

As you have burned the candle, give the inch 449

Take gifts with a sigh, most men give to be paid 450

O'Neill's gift and his two eyes looking after it (*see notes*) 451

It is worth going to meet generosity that is slow 452

GENTLENESS

A gentle answer quenches anger 453

A kind word never broke anyone's mouth 454

GOD

God's help is nearer than the door 455

God is not as severe as he is said to be 456

GOODNESS

GOSSIP

A whisper in Nora's ear is louder than a shout from the highest hill 476

A woman told me that a woman told her that she saw a woman who saw a woman who made ale of potatoes 477

The death of the old woman and the marriage of the young woman 478

Talk by the fire is the talk of idle women 479

GRATITUDE

Sit on your heel and thank goodness for a new stool 480

You can't examine the teeth of a gift horse 481

Eaten bread is soon forgotten 482

I think little of buttermilk when I'm full of it 483

Strike a dog with a bone and he'll not growl 484

Thank God the right side of the house is out 485

GREED

One cannot take out of a sack more than the full of it 486

If the cat had a churn her paw would often be in it 487

Though honey is sweet, do not lick it off a briar 488

The covetous man is always in want 489

He's not covetous but he'd fain have all 490

'Wide is the door of the little cottage'

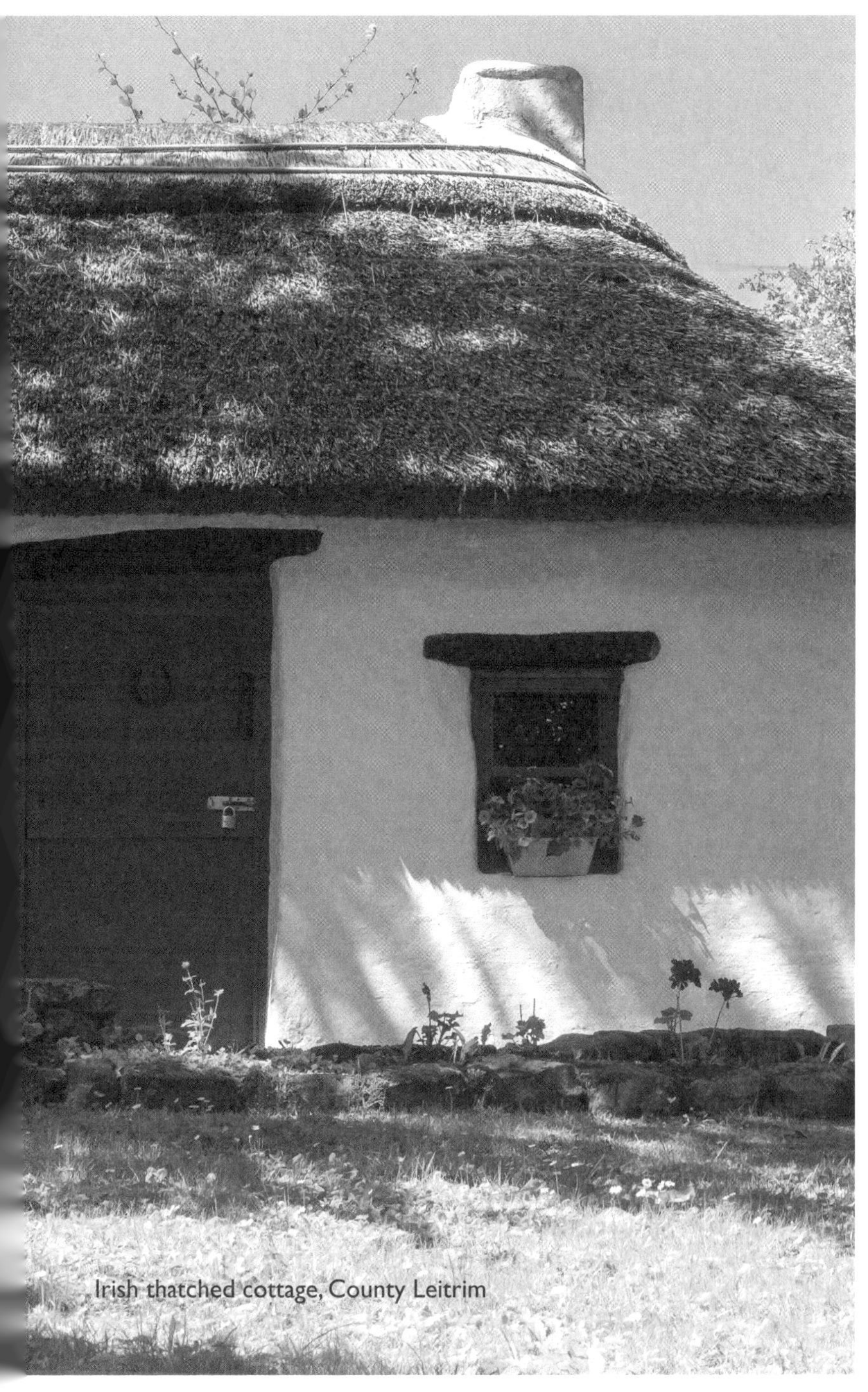
Irish thatched cottage, County Leitrim

GRIEF

HAPPINESS

HEALTH

A long disease doesn't tell a lie; it kills at last 505

Health is better than wealth 506

Health is better than flocks 507

A healthy man is a king 508

The relapse is worse than the final fever 509

Every patient is a doctor after his own cure 510

What butter or whiskey will not cure, there's no cure for 511

A long illness doesn't lie 512

Beginning with a cough and ending with a coffin 513

A graveyard cough 514

The person who doesn't scatter the morning dew will not comb grey hairs 515

One must pay health its tithes 516

The physician's hope, every misfortune 517

Patience is the cure for an old illness 518

HOME

There is no fireside like your own fireside 519

It's a long way from home that the plover cries 520

HONESTY

When rogues disagree, honest men get their own 521

The man that steals stacks thinks all the world thieves 522

The miller's pigs are fat but God knows whose meal they ate 523

He is as honest as the priest 524

HONOUR

A patch is better than a hole, but a hole is more honourable than a patch 525

It's more difficult to maintain honour than to become prosperous 526

A man may live after losing his life but not after losing his honour 527

Honour is more precious than gold 528

HOPE

Live horse and you'll get grass 529

Hope soothes the tired heart 530

Hope is the physician of each misery 531

Face the sun but turn your back on the storm 532

There's no flood that doesn't recede 533

Do not expect more than you deserve 534

God never sent a mouth without something with it 535

The dogs have not eaten up the end of the year yet 536

Good hope is better than a bad intention 537

There are fish in the tide as good as any that has been taken 538

There's fish in the sea better than was ever caught 539

In the end the improvement comes 540

The night and the day are as long as ever they were 541

HUMILITY

The last place is worthy of the best loved 542

The heaviest ear of corn is the one that lowest bends its head 543

HUMOUR

Good humour comes from the kitchen 544

Crying is not far away from laughter 545

HUNGER

It's a good story that fills the belly 546

Hunger is a good sauce 547

The mountain is a good mustard 548

The hungry hound thinks not of her whelps 549

Sharp is the eye of the hungry person 550

A blessing does not fill the stomach 551

IDLENESS

Talking never brought the turf home 552

Don't let the grass grow under your feet 553

Better idle than working for nothing 554

It is better to be putting knots on a straw than to be idle 555

A foot at rest meets nothing 556

You have the foal's share of the harrow 557

IGNORANCE

No ignorance in ordinance or law 558

IMPOSSIBILITY

The rod impossible to twist 559

INDEPENDENCE

Do your own job and eat your own fruits 560

INEQUALITY

What's rent to a lord is food to a child 561

A king's shilling is no more than a poor man's farthing 562

INITIATIVE

The army that attacks will not be attacked 563

The ebb-tide won't wait for the slow man 564

A shut fist will not catch a hawk 565

Strike the ball when you get it on the hop 566

Strike while the iron is hot 567

The man without resourcefulness is no better than a pig 568

INTELLIGENCE

A spur in the head is worth two on the heel 569

INVOLVEMENT

In for a penny, in for a pound 570

You might as well be hung for a sheep as a lamb 571

An inch is as good as a mile 572

IRISHMAN

An Irishman carries his heart in his hand 573

Put an Irishman on the spit and you'll find two more to turn him 574

An Irishman is never at peace except when he's fighting 575

The Irishman is impatient 576

JUDGEMENT

Don't make little of your dish for it may be an ignorant fellow who judges it 577

JUSTICE

KERRY

KINDNESS

KINSHIP

One pig knows another 592

One liar knows another 593

Great minds live apart, people may meet, but mountains and rocks never 594

KNOWLEDGE

A blind dog won't bark at the moon 595

A book to a blind man signifies nothing 596

Better knowledge of the evil, than the evil without knowledge 597

The person with least knowledge talks most 598

LAW

It's no joke going to law with the Devil and the court held in Hell 599

Beyond the leap, beyond the law 600

A good word in court is better than a pound in the purse 601

Neither break a law nor make one 602

The law does not apply to the blow that's not struck 603

The lying man's witness is his wife 604

LAZINESS

Winter comes fast on the lazy 605

Cold in the shoulder makes the shins speckled (*see notes*) 606

Long sleep makes a bare backside 607

It's only a worthless hen that fails to provide for herself 608

The speckled shins of spring is the envious one in autumn (*see notes*) 609

Laziness is a heavy burden 610

You'd be a good messenger to send for death 611

Pity the man who waits till the last day 612

Ye look for the ladle when the pot's in the fire 613

The long stitch of the lazy tailor 614

A slow messenger is the better for your going to meet him 615

It's a bad bird that dirties its own nest 616

It's a bad hen that won't scratch herself 617

LEADERSHIP

After the chieftains fall, the fight seldom continues 618

LIES

As great a liar as the clock of Strabane 619

The lie often goes further than the truth 620

God does not like the lying tongue 621

LIFE

We live as long as we're let 622

You will live during the year for we were just talking of you 623

Life is sweet 624

Life is precious 625

People live in one another's shadows 626

Twenty years agrowing; twenty years at rest; twenty years declining; and twenty years when it doesn't matter whether you're there or not 627

Life is the true historian 628

LOVE

Live in my heart and pay no rent 629

If you love the mother, you love her brood 630

They won't fall in love with the man they don't see 631

When the sight leaves the eye, love leaves the heart 632

After the settlement (the dowry) comes the love 633

Love is blind to blemishes and faults 634

Love hides ignominy and evil 635

Love is no impartial judge 636

House without hound, cat, or child, house without love or affection 637

Love a woman or a child without their knowing it 638

To the raven her own chick is white 639

What is nearest the heart is usually nearest the lips 640

What is nearest the heart comes out 641

Love cools quickly 642

Love conceals ugliness, and hate sees a lot of faults 643

She who fills the heart fills the eye 644

There's no love until there's a family 645

Absence makes the heart grow fond 646

LUCK

It's better to be lucky than to be an early riser 647

A chance shot will not kill the Devil 648

The man who has luck in the morning has luck in the afternoon 649

There's luck in sharing 650

It's better to be lucky than wise 651

A meeting in the sunlight is lucky, and a burying in the rain 652

The lucky person has only to be born 653

Luck seldom lasts 654

MANNERS

Without store no friends; without rearing no manners 655

Better good manners than good looks 656

MARRIAGE

The husband of the sloven is known in the field amidst a crowd 657

A growing moon and a flowing tide are lucky times to marry in 658

Never make a toil of pleasure, as the man said when he dug his wife's grave only three feet deep 659

Marriage at the dungheap and the godparents far away 660

Woe to him who does not heed a good wife's counsel 661

It's why women marry … the creatures, God bless them, are too shy to say no 662

There was never an old slipper but there was an old stocking to match it 663

A young man is bothered till he's married; after that he's bothered entirely 664

There's only one thing in the world better than a good wife … no wife 665

The dowry falls over the cliff; but the protruding lip remains on the wife 666

A bad wife takes advice from everyone but her husband 667

'Winter comes fast on the lazy'

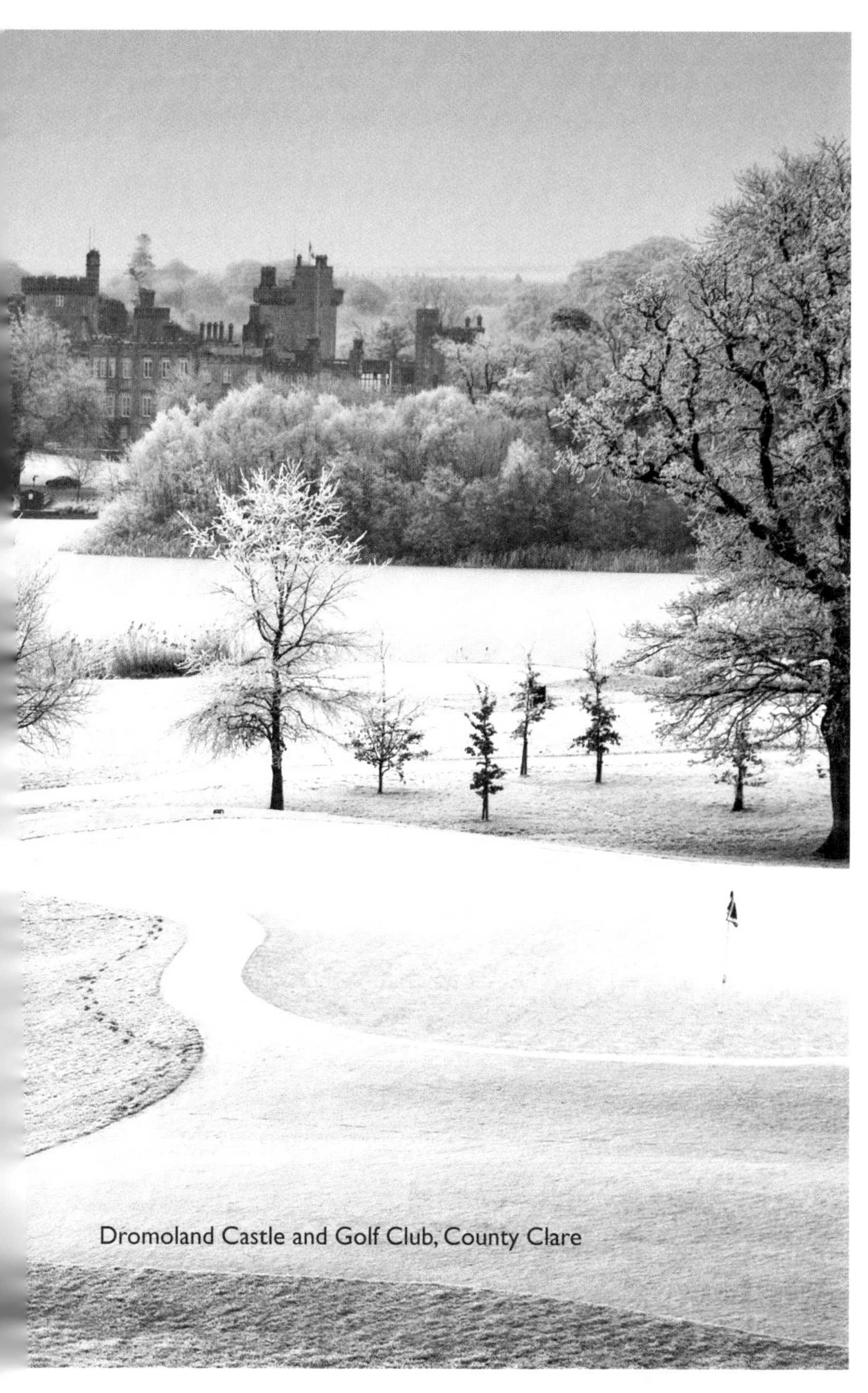

Dromoland Castle and Golf Club, County Clare

He breaks his wife's head and then buys a plaster for it 668

There are no trials till marriage 669

The carefree mother's daughter makes a bad wife 670

It's a lonesome washing that there's not a (man's) shirt in 671

Marry a mountainy woman and you'll marry the mountain 672

She's a good woman, but she didn't take off her boots yet 673

The day you marry your wife you marry your children 674

The blanket is the warmer of being doubled 675

She burnt her coal and did not warm herself 676

He married money and got a woman with it 677

Marry in haste and be sorry at your leisure 678

MATURITY

By age or ability you're no child 679

MEANNESS

What you give wouldn't blind the eye of a midge 680

As tight as tuppence in a market-woman's trashbag 681

If you give the loan of your britches, don't cut off the buttons 682

'Tis strange that the man who is so quick to find fault is himself so stingy about food 683

MEN

MISFORTUNE

MOTHER

A mother with a pouch is better than a father with a ploughteam 699

NATURE

You won't get from a cat but its skin 700

The lamb is a sheep in the long run 701

Its nature breaks out through the eyes of the cat 702

Let the tail go with the hide 703

A wild goose never laid a tame egg 704

What can you expect from a pig but a grunt 705

How could the apple be but like the apple tree 706

Nature is stronger than nurture 707

He got it from nature as the pig got the rooting in the ground 708

Often a cow does not take after its breed 709

What would a young cat do but eat mice? 710

Nature will come through the claws, and the hound will follow the hare 711

If you put a silk dress on a goat he is a goat still 712

Every bird as it is reared and the lark for the bog 713

What is in the marrow is hard to take out of the bone 714

The wood will renew the foliage it sheds 715

What will come from the briar but the berry 716

The hand goes only where the leg goes 717

NEATNESS

A handstaff of holly, a *buailtín* of hazel, a single sheaf and a clean floor (*see notes*) 718

NECESSITY

One who is without cows must be his own dog 719

Make necessity a virtue 720

Necessity accepts no law 721

A blind man can see his mouth 722

You never miss the water till the well has run dry 723

NOBILITY

A king's son is not nobler than his food 724

OBEDIENCE

Keep your tongue in your jaw and your toe in your pump 725

OBLIGATION

Pity the man who has a stranger's spancel on him 726

OWNERSHIP

To every cow its calf; to every book its copy (*see notes*) 727

PARTICIPATION

Watching is a part of good play 728

PATIENCE

By degrees the castles are built 729

When the apple is ripe, it will fall 730

Patience cures many an old complaint 731

The one who waits the fine day will get the fine day 732

Patience and forbearance made a bishop of his reverence 733

Patience can conquer destiny 734

Patience is a plaster for all sores 735

For what cannot be cured patience is best 736

There is not a tree in Heaven higher than the tree of patience 737

Patience is a virtue that causes no shame 738

Time and patience would bring the snail to Jerusalem 739

PATRIOTISM

Everyone praises his native land 740

PEACE

Nobody ever bought peace but the man who hadn't got it 741

Peace (quietness) is worth buying 742

The world's quiet and the pig is in the sty 743

Least said soonest mended 744

No matter who succeeds or fails, the peacemaker will always suffer 745

To the fighting man peace is sure 746

The end of a feast is better than the beginning of a fight 747

PERCEPTION

An eye is blind in another man's corner 748

One eye in the corner is sharper than two about the house 749

PITY

He's more to be pitied than laughed at 750

Don't tell your complaint to one who has no pity 751

POETRY

A poem ought to be well made at first, for there is many a one to spoil it afterwards 752

POSSESSION

It's better than it's want 753

Have it yourself, or else do without it 754

Better the certainty of the straddle (packsaddle) than the mere loan of a saddle 755

Possession is nine-tenths of the law 756

Better own a trifle than want a great deal 757

A wren in the hand is better than a crane to be caught 758

Possession satisfies 759

A bird in the hand is worth two in the bush 760

It's better than the loan you couldn't get 761

Half a loaf is better than no bread 762

A live dog is better than a dead lion 763

A trout in the pot is better than a salmon in the sea 764

POVERTY

Put a beggar on horseback and he'll ride to Hell 765

Put a beggar on horseback and he'll go on a gallop 766

Poverty parts good company 767

Poverty destroys companionship 768

Many a defect is seen in the poor man 769

It's hard to take britches off bare hips 770

The full man does not understand the wants of the hungry 771

A little pleases a poor man 772

Poor men take to the sea; the rich to the mountains 773

Poverty creates sadness 774

Pity the man who does wrong and is poor as well 775

There is nothing in the world so poor as going to Hell 776

The thief is no danger to the beggar 777

Poverty is no shame 778

Two things that go to loss: turf on a mountain and the wisdom of a poor man 779

Shame is ever a part of poverty 780

No one is ever poor who has the sight of his eyes and the use of his feet 781

There is no tune without a penny 782

A poor man never yet lost his property 783

Poor is the church without music 784

A smokey cabin, a handful of spuds and a flea-filled bed 785

POWER

No stopping the force of a going wheel by hand 786

No forcing the sea 787

PRESUMPTION

Don't count your chickens before they are hatched 788

Don't bless the fish till it gets to the land 789

Don't build the sty until the litter comes 790

Praise the ripe field not the green corn 791

Praise the ford when you have crossed it 792

You must empty a box before you fill it again 793

PRIDE

The pride of women and the pride of priests 794

It is difficult to soothe the proud 795

Pride comes before a fall 796

Pride feels no pain 797

Pride is the author of every sin 798

The jump of a cock on the dungheap 799

PROCRASTINATION

There is no virtue in the herb that is not got in time 800

A postponement till morning, a postponement for ever 801

It is no time to go for the doctor when the patient is dead 802

PROMISE

A promise is a debt 803

PROVERBS

Proverbs cannot be contradicted 804

The proverb cannot be bettered 805

Though the proverb is abandoned, it is not falsified 806

PRUDENCE

Don't throw out the dirty water until you have the clean water in 807

It's better to return from the centre of the ford than drown in the flood 808

The sty before the litter 809

RED HAIR

If you meet a red-haired woman, you'll meet a crowd 810

To be red-haired is better than to be without a head 811

REPENTANCE

To put off repentance is dangerous 812

It's better to be sorry and stay than to be sorry and go away 813

REPUTATION

It's a small thing that outlives a man 814

Remember even if you lose all, keep your good name, for if you lose that you are worthless 815

Those who get the name of rising early may lie all day 816

When a man gets his feet in the lime he cannot easily get rid of it 817

REVENGE

No dealing with a revengeful man 818

ROGUE

He was never good since the time a yard (of cloth) made a coat for him 819

Don't mention him and a decent man in the one day 820

A sly rogue is often in good dress 821

She would drink the cream and say the cat she had was an old rogue 822

The horse with the most scars is the one that highest kicks his rear 823

RUMOUR

The person who brings a story to you will take away two from you 824

A story without an author is not worth listening to 825

Leave the bad tale where you found it 826

There is no smoke without fire 827

SCARCITY

When all fruits fail, welcome haws 828

When the fruit is scarcest, its taste is sweetest 829

We have a fine day more often than a kiln-cast 830

SEASONS

A soft-dropping April brings milk to cows and sheep 831

Autumn days come quickly like the running of a hound on the moor 832

A misty winter brings a pleasant spring, a pleasant winter a misty spring 833

Many a sudden change takes place on a spring day 834

In winter the milk goes to the cow's horns 835

SECRET

A secret is a weapon and a friend 836

It is no secret that is known to three 837

Fences (ditches) have ears 838

Don't tell your secret even to a fence 839

Woe to the man that entrusts his secrets to a ditch 840

The secret of an old woman scolding 841

If it's a secret, it's binding 842

Don't tell secrets to the children of your relatives 843

'No forcing the sea'

Cliffs of Moher, County Clare

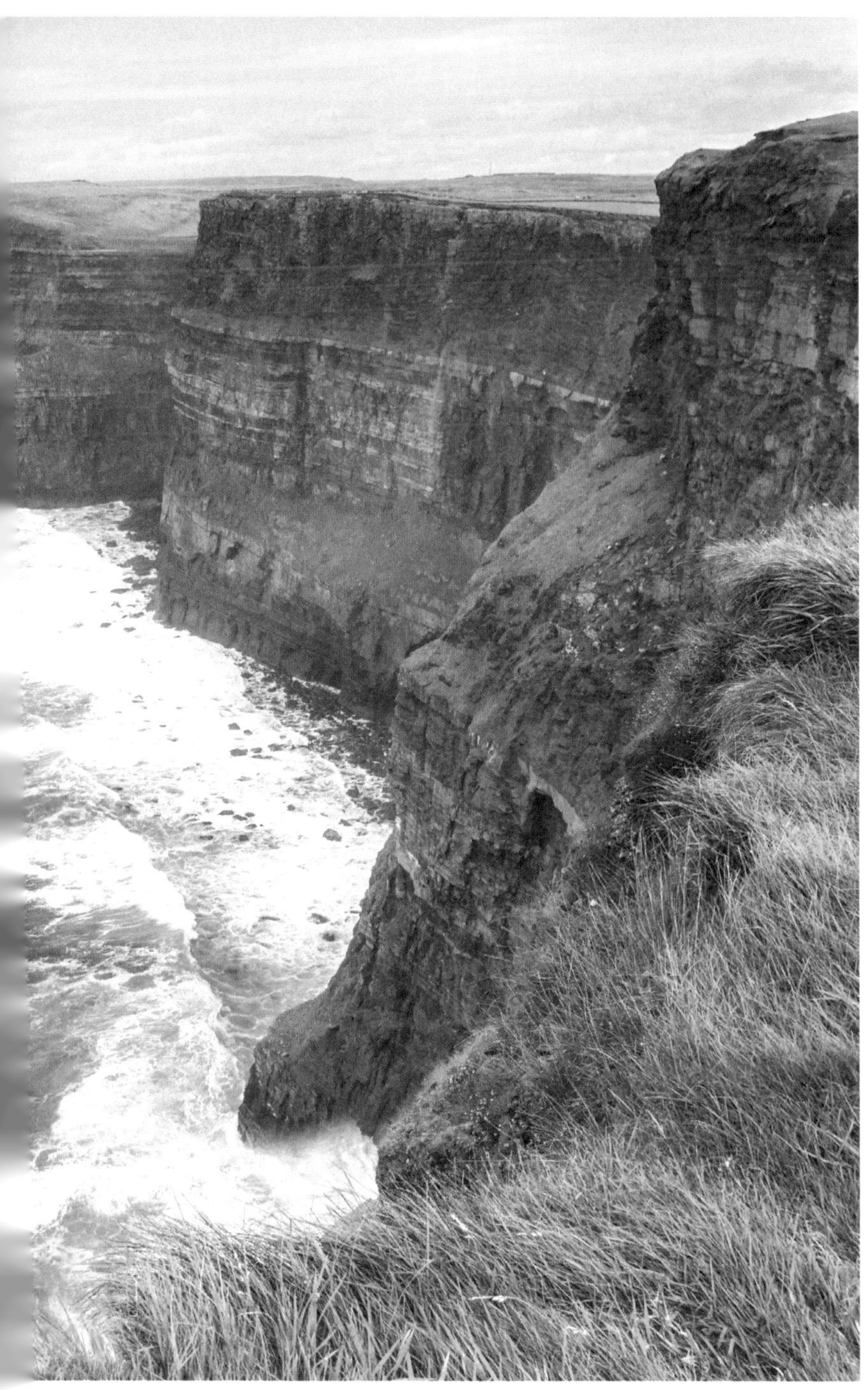

SELF-DESTRUCTION

No tree but has rotten wood enough to burn it 844

A man may be his own ruin 845

A wedge from itself splits the oak tree 846

A man has often cut a rod to beat himself 847

SELFISHNESS

It's for her own good that the cat purrs 848

His own wound is what everyone feels soonest 849

What is nearest the heart is nearest the mouth 850

He who is best to me is he who shall get the best share 851

The full stomach does not understand the empty one 852

The man who was dividing Ireland didn't leave himself last 853

SENSE

Sense doesn't come before age 854

SEPARATION

After the gathering comes the scattering 855

SHAME

What would shame him would turn back a funeral 856

A fist full of gain and a village full of shame 857

Better is the trouble that follows death than the trouble that follows shame 858

SHYNESS

Do not keep your tongue under your belt 859

A man is shy in another man's corner 860

SILENCE

A silent mouth is musical 861

The silent are often guilty 862

The silent mouth is sweet to hear 863

When wrathful words arise, a closed mouth is soothing 864

The stars make no noise 865

Little talk is easy to cure 866

A closed mouth … a wise head 867

A silent mouth never did any harm 868

STRENGTH

Strength is not enduring 869

STUPIDITY

Sending the goose on a message to the fox's den 870

Putting the fox to mind the geese 871

You didn't turn up when sense was being distributed 872

SUCCESS

There's neither success nor efficiency without authority and laws 873

Fat is not to be had without labour 874

SUITABILITY

The windy day is not the day for thatching 875

One's man meat is another man's poison 876

Whoever the cap fits takes it 877

TACT

Better sit beside him than in his place 878

A short visit is best and that not too often 879

The eye should be blind in the home of another 880

It's often a man's mouth broke his nose 881

Don't say everything you want to say lest you hear something you would not like to hear 882

Don't let your tongue cut your throat 883

See not what you see and hear not what you hear 884

Never speak to the feet while the head is alive 885

Don't rest your eyes beyond what is your own 886

It's bad manners to talk about ropes in the house of a man whose father was hanged 887

TALENT

A greyhound finds food in its feet 888

The slow hound often has good qualities 889

The bird that can sing and won't sing should be made to sing 890

A cat between two houses, a rabbit between two holes, the two liveliest 891

TALKATIVENESS

Great talk and little action 892

Do not be talkative in an alehouse 893

You kissed the blarney stone 894

THRIFT

A spender gets the property of the hoarder 895

Let your bargain suit your purpose 896

Spread your cloth only as you can draw it 897

TIME

The waiting man thinks the time long 898

A watched kettle never boils 899

Time is a good storyteller 900

TREACHERY

He who spies is the one who kills 901

Treachery returns 902

TROUBLE

There's trouble in every house and some in the street 903

Everything troubles you and the cat breaks your heart 904

TRUST

The fox never found a better messenger than himself 905

Never trust a spiteful man 906

TRUTH

A man with a loud laugh makes truth itself seem folly 907

Truth is great and will win out 908

Even the truth may be bitter 909

There are two tellings to every story 910

Drunkenness and anger 'tis said tell the truth 911

What I'm afraid to hear I'd better say first myself 912

Truth speaks even though the tongue were dead 913

You can keep away from the rogue, but you cannot keep yourself safe from the liar 914

Truth stands when everything else falls 915

It is no shame to tell the truth 916

Tell the truth and shame the Devil 917

UNDERSTANDING

The well-filled belly has little understanding of the empty 918

'Tis afterwards that everything is understood 919

USELESSNESS

It's a bad hound that's not worth the whistling 920

He knows how many grains to a bushel of wheat 921

He knows the price of everything and the value of nothing 922

He couldn't drag a herring off the coals 923

It's just a wisp in place of a brush 924

VALUE

One pair of good soles is worth two pairs of upper leathers 925

Without pressing too little or too hard, hold tight the reins for he's a fool who would not get value from a borrowed horse 926

It's not worth a cuckoo-spit 927

Better an idle house than a bad tenant 928

VANITY

Pity him who makes his opinion a certainty 929

He thinks that he himself is the very stone that was hurled at the castle 930

He dotes on his midden and thinks it the moon 931

WARNING

That's a spoon ye'll sup sorrow with yet 932

WASTEFULNESS

Wilful waste makes woeful want 933

WEALTH

A shamefaced man seldom acquires wealth 934

The money-maker (profiteer) is never tired 935

The doorstep of a great house is slippery 936

There is misfortune only where there is wealth 937

Sweet is the voice of the man who has wealth 938

A hut is a palace to a poor man 939

A heavy purse makes a light heart 940

There's little value in the single cow 941

A man of one cow – a man of no cow 942

It's easy to knead when meal is at hand 943

WEATHER

Wind from the east is good for neither man nor beast 944

A Kerry shower is of twenty-four hours 945

Better April showers than the breadth of the ocean in gold 946

WELCOME

Better for a man to have even a dog welcome him than a dog bark at him 947

Going in is not the same as going out 948

A welcome is a debtor's face 949

WIDOW

What's all the world to a man when his wife is a widow 950

WISDOM

A wise head keeps a shut mouth 951

Everyone is wise till he speaks 952

Food is no more important than wisdom 953

A contraction (in writing) is enough for a scholar 954

The beginning of wisdom is the fear of God 955

There's no wise man without a fault 956

He may die of wind but he'll never die of wisdom 957

You can't put a wise head on young shoulders 958

Wisdom is what makes a poor man a king, a weak person powerful, a good generation of a bad one, a foolish man reasonable 959

Though wisdom is good in the beginning, it is better at the end 960

A little of anything isn't worth a pin, but a wee bit of sense is worth a lot 961

No making of a wise man 962

WOMEN

A dishonest woman can't be kept in, and an honest woman won't 963

There is no thing wickeder than a woman of evil temper 964

A bad woman (/wife) drinks a lot of her own bad butter-milk 965

A foolish woman knows a foolish man's faults 966

A whistling woman and a crowing hen will bring no luck to the house they are in 967

Beef to the heels like a Mullingar heifer 968

Eight lives for the men and nine for the women 969

Wherever there are women there's talking, and wherever there's geese there's cackling 970

Irishwomen have a dispensation from the Pope to wear the thick ends of their legs downwards 971

Women are shy and shame prevents them from refusing a man 972

Everything dear is a woman's fancy 973

Like an Irish wolf she barks at her own shadow 974

She wipes the plate with the cat's tail 975

More hair than tit, like a mountain heifer 976

Women are stronger than men, they do not die of wisdom 977

When the old woman is hard pressed, she has to run 978

It's difficult to trust a woman 979

Man to the hills, woman to the shore 980

Beat a woman with a hammer and you'll have gold 981

'Tis as hard to see a woman cry as a goose go barefoot 982

'Where comes a cow', the wise man [St Colmcille] lay down, 'there follows a woman, and where comes a woman follows trouble' 983

Only a fool would prefer food to a woman 984

Don't be ever in court or a castle without a woman to make your excuse 985

An excuse is nearer to a woman than her apron 986

There is nothing sharper than a woman's tongue 987

A woman without is she who has neither pipe nor child 988

The yellow *praiseach* (kale) of the fields that brings the Meath women to harm 989

A woman like a goose, a sharp pecking woman
A woman like a pig, a sleepy-headed woman
A woman like a sickle, a strong stubborn woman
A woman like a goat, a woman of rushing visits
A woman like a sheep, an affable friendly woman
A woman like a lamb, a quiet friendly woman 990

It is not the most beautiful woman who has the most sense 991

A woman can beat the Devil 992

A shrew gets her wish but suffers in the getting 993

WORK

Many a time, the man with ten (cows) has overtaken the man with forty (cows) 994

Do it as if there were fire in your skin 995

The seeking for one thing will find another 996

Make your hay before the fine weather leaves you 997

Sow early and mow early 998

The early riser gets through his business but not through early rising 999

The slow horse reaches the mill 1000

Making the beginning is one third of the work 1001

The quiet pigs eat all the draff 1002

The sweat of one's brow is what burns everyone 1003

Everyone lays a burden on the willing horse 1004

Every little makes a mickle 1005

Speed and accuracy do not agree 1006

Never put off tomorrow what you can do today 1007

I'll go there tonight for evening is speedier than morning 1008

The person of the greatest talk is the person of the least work 1009

Be there with the day and be gone with the day 1010

About evening a man is known 1011

Long churning makes bad butter 1012

Scattering is easier than gathering 1013

The labour of the crow 1014

Put it on your shoulder and say it is not a burden 1015

It's no delay to stop to edge the tool 1016

The mason who strikes often is better than the one who strikes too hard 1017

It destroys the craft not to learn it 1018

The dog that's always on the go is better than the one that's always curled up 1019

Handfuls make a load 1020

Don't go early or late to the well 1021

A good beginning is half the work 1022

YOUTH

Praise the young and they will make progress 1023

Many a shabby colt makes a fine horse 1024

The young shed many skins 1025

Youth likes to wander 1026

The growth of the gosling 1027

Youth cannot believe 1028

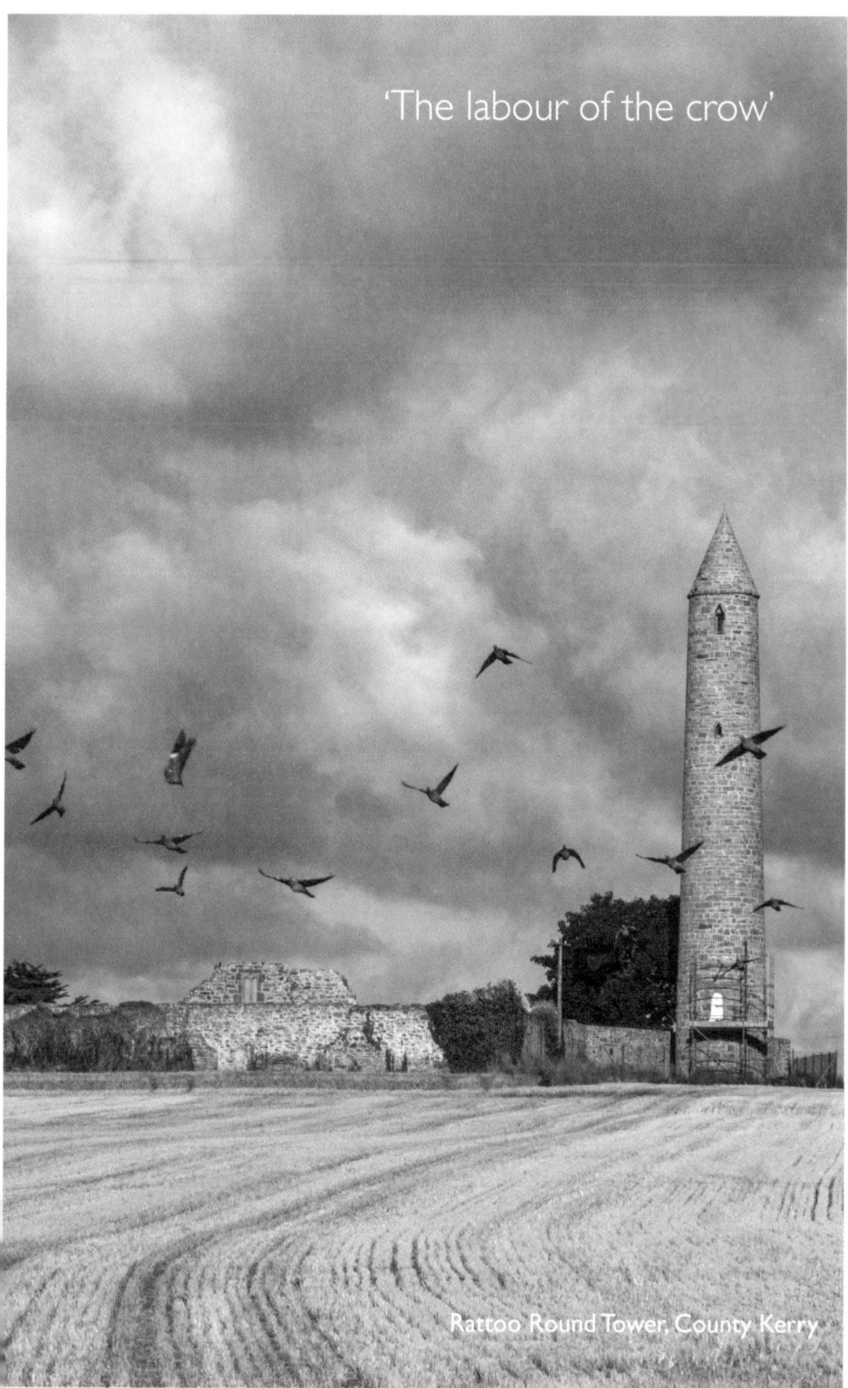

'The labour of the crow'

Rattoo Round Tower, County Kerry

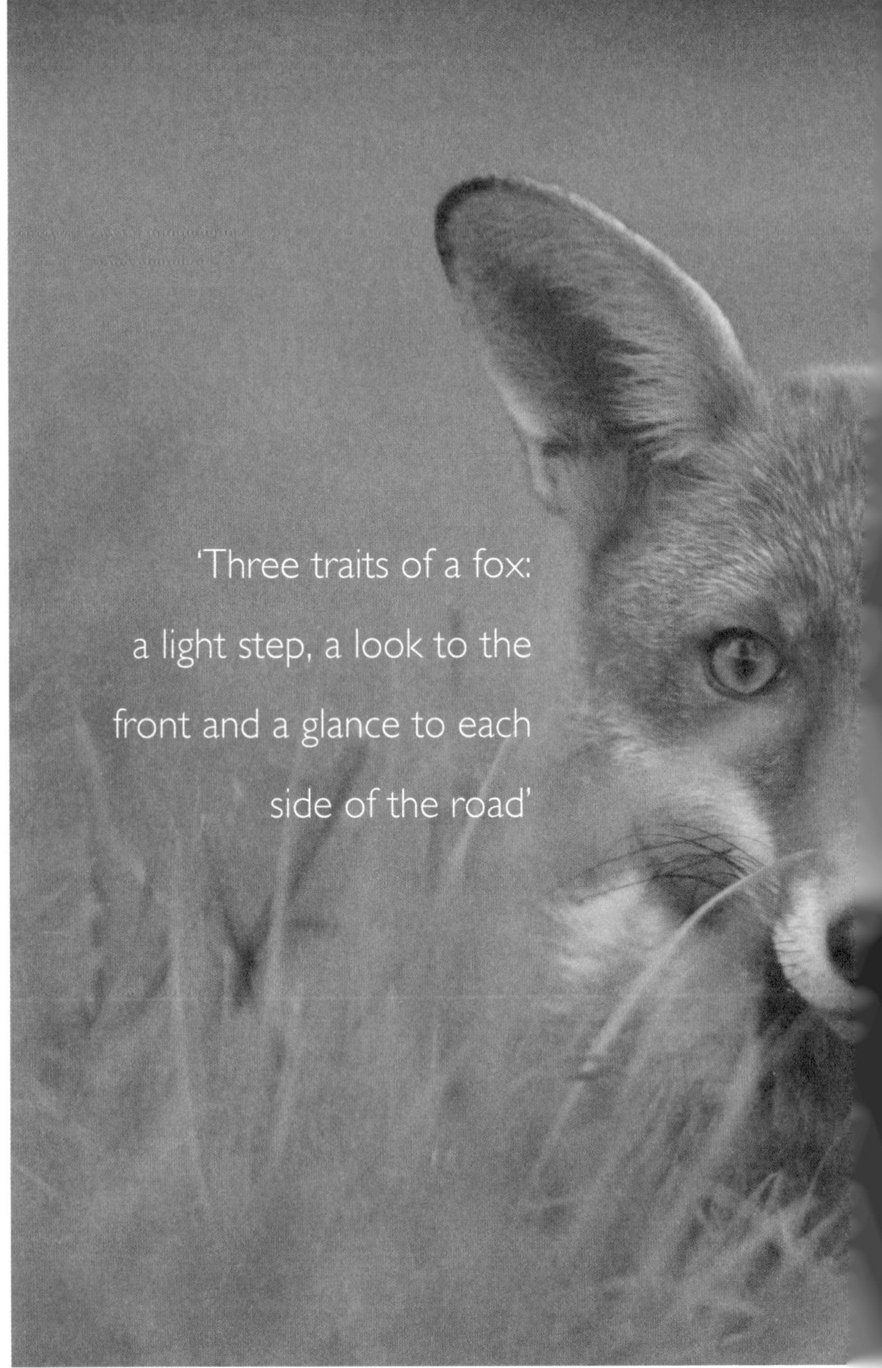
'Three traits of a fox:
a light step, a look to the
front and a glance to each
side of the road'

TRIADS

THREE AS GOOD AS

Three things as good as the best: dirty water to quench a fire, a frieze coat on a frosty day and black bread in famine time 1029

Three things that are as good as things better than them: a wooden sword in a coward's hand, an ugly wife married to a blind man and poor clothes on a drunken man 1030

THREE BEST

Three best friends and three worst enemies: fire, wind and rain 1031

Three best to have in plenty: sunshine, wisdom and generosity 1032

Three best things to have a surplus of: money after paying the rent, seed after spring and friends at home 1033

Three best invitations: come to mass, come and make secure and come to the mill 1034

Three with best sight: the eye of a blacksmith on a nail, the eye of a young girl at a contest and the eye of a priest on his parish 1035

Three best small: a beehive, a sheep and a woman 1036

The three best sounds: the sound of the flail, the sound of the quern, the sound of the churn 1037

THREE FORTUNES

The three fortunes of the cat: the housewife's forgetfulness, walking without a sound and keen sight in darkness 1038

Three fortunes of the lucky man: fences, vigilance and early rising 1039

Three fortunes of the unlucky man: long visits to his neighbours, long morning sleep and bad fences 1040

THREE HARDEST

The three hardest to go through: a waterfall, a bog and a briary track 1041

The three hardest to select: a Sunday woman, an autumn sheep and an old mare's foal 1042

THREE KINDS

The three kinds of brain: brain as hard as stone, brain as receptive as wax and brain as unstable as flowing water 1043

The three kinds of men: the worker, the pleasure-seeker and the boaster 1044

The three kinds of men who fail to understand women: young men, old men and middle-aged men 1045

The three kinds of men who rise earliest: the husband of a talkative wife, the man with a stolen white horse and the man with the dirty tattered shirt 1046

The three kinds of poor people: the man poor by the will of God, the man poor by his own will and the man poor even if he owned the world 1047

The three kinds of women: the woman as shameless as a pig, the woman as unruly as a hen and the woman as gentle as a lamb 1048

THREE MOST

Three most bothersome things in the world: a thorn in the foot, a woman and a goat going to the fair that will go any way but the way you want it 1049

The three most delightful things to see: a garden of white potatoes covered in blossom, a ship under sail and a woman after giving birth 1050

The three most difficult to select: a woman, a scythe and a razor 1051

The three most difficult to teach: a mule, a pig and a woman 1052

The three most difficult to understand: the mind of a woman, the labour of the bees and the ebb and flow of the tide 1053

The three most fortunate things a man ever had: a mare, a sow and a goose 1054

The three most nourishing foods: beef marrow, the flesh of a chicken, Scandinavian beer 1055

The three most pleasant things: a cat's kitten, a goat's kid and a young widow-woman 1056

The three most troubled eyes: the eye of a blacksmith after the nail, the eye of a chicken after the grain and the eye of a girl seeking her sweetheart 1057

THREE TRAITS

Three traits of a bull: a bold walk, a strong neck and a hard forehead 1058

Three traits of a fox: a light step, a look to the front and a glance to each side of the road 1059

Three traits of a hare: a lively ear, a bright eye and a quick run against the hill 1060

Three traits of a woman: a broad bosom, a slender waist and a short back 1061

THREE UGLIEST

The three ugliest things that are: a hairless mangy dog, a woman without flesh or blood and a deceitful, shameless girl 1062

The three ugliest things of their own kind: a thin red-haired woman, a thin yellow horse and a thin white cow 1063

THREE USELESS

The three things useless when old: an old schoolmaster, an old horse and an old soldier 1064

Three things that are of little use: a trumpet and no tongue, a button and no buttonhole and a wolf without teeth 1065

THREE WORST

The three worst departures: leaving mass before it ends, leaving table without grace and leaving your wife to go to another woman 1066

The three worst endings: the last days of a noble old lady, the last days of an old white horse and the last days of an old schoolmaster 1067

The three worst endings: a house burning, a ship sinking and an old white horse dying 1068

The three worst pets: a pet priest, a pet beggar and a pet pig 1069

The three worst things to have in a house: a scolding wife, a smokey chimney and a leaky roof 1070

The three worse things of all: small, soft potatoes, from that to an uncomfortable bed and to sleep with a bad woman 1071

THREE THINGS

The things that cannot be acquired: voice, generosity and poetry 1072

Three things that arrive unnoticed: rent, age and a beard 1073

Three things to beware of: the hoof of the horse, the horn of the bull and the smile of the Saxon (*see notes*) 1074

Three things a man should not boast of: the size of his purse, the beauty of his wife and the sweetness of his beer 1075

Three things bright at first, then dull and finally black: co-operation, a marriage alliance and living in the one house 1076

Three things Christ never intended: a woman whistling, a hound howling and a hen crowing 1077

Three things that relate to drink: to pay for it, to drink it and to carry it 1078

Three things that fill a haggard: ambition, industry and constant vigilance 1079

Three good things to have: a clean shirt, a clean conscience and a guinea in the pocket 1080

Three disagreeable things at home: a scolding wife, a squalling child and a smoky chimney 1081

Three things that don't bear nursing: an old woman, a hen and a sheep 1082

Three things that are purposeless: throwing a stone on a bend, giving advice to a wrathful woman, talking to a head without sense 1083

Three things that remain longest in a family: fighting, red hair and thieving 1084

Three things that don't remain: a white cow, a handsome woman and a house on a height 1085

Three things that can never return: a Sunday without mass, a day away from school and a day away from work 1086

Three things that won't have rest: a steep waterfall, an otter and a devil out of Hell 1087

Three things that never rust: a woman's tongue, the shoes of a butcher's horse and charitable people's money 1088

Three things that never rust: a sword, a spade and a thought 1089

Three things never seen: a blade's edge, wind and love 1090

Three sharpest things that are: a hound's tooth, a thorn in the mud and a fool's word 1091

The three sharpest things: a fool's word, a thorn in the mud and a soft woollen thread that cuts to the bone 1092

Three things that survive for the shortest time: a woman's association, the love of a mare for her foal and fresh oaten bread 1093

Three thing swiftest in the sea: the seal, the ray and the mackerel 1094

Three things swiftest on land: the hound, the hare and the fox 1095

Three things that leave the shortest traces: a bird on a branch, a ship on the sea and a man on a woman 1096

Three things that leave the longest traces: charcoal on wood, a chisel on a block of stone and a ploughshare on a furrow 1097

Three things not to be trusted: a fine day in winter, the life of an old person or the word of an important man unless it's in writing 1098

Three things not be trusted: a cow's horn, a dog's tooth and a horse's hoof 1099

Three things of least value in any house: too many geese in a house without a lake, too many women in a house without wool to be spun, too many horses in a house without ploughing to be done 1100

Three things that have little value: the head of a woodcock, the head of a goat and the head of a gurnet 1101

Three things a man should not be without: a cat, a chimney and a housewife 1102

MISCELLANEOUS

Three parts of the body most easily hurt: the knee, the elbow and the eye 1103

Three that do not clean their snouts: the farmer, the dog and the pig 1104

Three coldest things that are: a hound's snout, a man's knee and a woman's breast 1105

Three to whom it's little sense to pay a compliment: an old man, a bad man and a child 1106

Three deaths that ought not be bemoaned: the death of a fat hog, the death of a thief and the death of a proud prince 1107

Three the Devil has without much trouble: the mason, the bailiff and the miller 1108

Three enemies of the body: wind, smoke and fleas 1109

Three errors relating to corn: to cut it green, to grind it damp and to eat it fresh 1110

Three great evils: smallness of house, closeness of heart and shortage of food 1111

Three with the sharpest eyes: a hawk on a tree, a fox in a glen, a young girl at a meeting 1112

Three wholesome foods for the driver: the back of a herring, the belly of a salmon and the head of a thrush (/moorhen) 1113

Three bad habits: drinking the glass, smoking the pipe and scattering the dew late at night 1114

Three happiest in the world: the tailor, the piper and the goat 1115

Three strokes that are keeping Ireland: the stroke of an axe on a block, of a hammer on an anvil and of a threshing flail in the centre 1116

Three jobs that must be done with vigour: rowing, hammering and measuring the ground with your fist (i.e. using the sickle) 1117

Three kind acts unrequited: that done for an old man, for a wicked person or for a little child 1118

Three sweetest melodies: the churning of butter, the plough ploughing and the mill grinding 1119

Three oaths that money swore: that it did not care who would possess it, that it would stay but a while with any man and that it would not stay with any man but the man who loved it 1120

Three pair that never agree: two married women in the same house, two cats with one mouse and two bachelors after the one young woman 1121

Three places that cannot be avoided: the place of birth, the place of death and the place of burial 1122

Three times it is most likely to rain: early on Friday, late on Saturday and on Sunday morning when it's time for first mass 1123

Three greatest rushes: the rush of water, the rush of fire and the rush of falsehood 1124

Three sauciest by nature: a ram, a bull and a tailor 1125

Three skills of the hare: sharp turning, high jumping and strong running against the hill 1126

Three strongest forces: the force of fire, the force of water and the force of hatred 1127

Three truths: sunrise, sunset and death 1128

Three unluckiest things to meet first thing in the morning: a mad dog, a man who lent you money and a red-haired girl 1129

Three virtues of the drunkard: a miserable morning, a dirty coat and an empty pocket 1130

Three signs of an unfortunate man: going bail, intervening in disputes and giving evidence 1131

The three characteristics of the Fianna: purity of heart, strength of limb and acting according to our word 1132

'Three truths:
sunrise, sunset and death'
The Great Sugarloaf Mountain, County Wicklow

‘The cat is his own best adviser’

FOURSOMES

FOURSOMES

Four priests who are not greedy; four Frenchmen who are not yellow (cowardly); four cobblers who don't tell lies; that's twelve not in this country 1133

Four things an Irishman should not trust: a cow's horn, a horse's hoof, a dog's snarl and an Englishman's laugh (*compare no. 1074*) 1134

The four fortunes of the cat: the housewife's error, walking without care, no water in milk and sight at night as well as by day (*compare no. 1038*) 1135

Four hateful things: a worthless hound, a slow horse, a chief without wisdom and a wife without children 1136

NOTES

Proverb 51

The *builtín* is the Irish word for the part of the flail that strikes the corn.

Proverb 52

Ciotóg is the Irish word for a left-handed person; it often implies awkwardness. In this instance, however, the implication is one of the cuteness or guile. Various superstitions have been associated with the *ciotóg* – including suspicion of evil or treachery (note the English word 'sinister', from the Latin).

Proverb 56

The Irish word *meitheal* means a team of workers (neighbours) assisting one another at turf-cutting or hay-making. The blacksmith usually had the largest *meitheal* in the parish since his work at the forge was of such importance to the community.

Proverb 61

'The Old Woman of Beare': a legendary figure in Irish folklore and poetry. (See Patrick Pearse's poem, 'Mise Eire' and Austin Clarke's 'The Young Woman of Beare'.)

Proverb 72

About AD 300, when Cormac mac Airt was High King of Ireland, ruling from Tara, a warrior army called the Fianna was formed under the leadership of Fionn mac Cumhaill. Around the Fianna and its leader grew a great body of legend still popular today. Fionn himself was noted for his bravery and wisdom (he tasted the salmon of knowledge). The

Fianna eventually became too powerful for the High King but were defeated at the battle of Gabhra and disbanded.

Proverb 208

The word 'cess', according to P. W. Joyce, may mean a contraction of success, or a 'contribution'. He refers to its use in County Louth as meaning a quantity of corn in for threshing.

Proverb 279

Lough Sheelin is a large lake in County Cavan.

Proverb 451

Used as a reply when you are reminded by someone of a favour they have granted you.

Proverb 606 and 609

'Speckled' refers to the 'heat-spots' got on the shins from sitting too long and too close by the fire.

Proverb 718

For *buailtín*, see note under proverb 51 above.

Proverb 727

This proverb is King Diarmuid's famous judgement, given about AD 560, on the ownership of a manuscript copy made by St Colmcille of a manuscript belonging to St Finnian. It must be one of our first copyright laws.

Proverb 1074

Another shorter, blunt saying affirms the fear and mistrust of the occupying English colonists: 'Beware the Sassanach.'

INDEX

obrien.ie